Glimpses of Architecture in Kerala

Temples and Palaces

Temple at Mannar

The temple at Mannar, close to Haripad,
in Kottayam district is a simple yet elegant
example of Kerala temple architecture.
Set just off the main road, the change
between the chaos outside and the
tranquillity inside is very rapid.
It represents that in life's turmoil, there
is a space for peace and stillness.

Text copyright © Ramu Katakam 2006
Photographs copyright © Joginder Singh and Ramu Katakam

Published 2006 by

Rupa & Co

7/16, Ansari Road, Daryaganj
New Delhi 110 002

Sales Centres:
Allahabad Bangalore Chandigarh
Chennai Hyderabad Jaipur Kathmandu
Kolkata Mumbai Pune

Design: Alpana Khare

Printed in India by
Ajanta Offset & Packaging Ltd
New Delhi-110 002

Readers are invited to send their comments to
ramu@katakam.com
jogisingh@gmail.com

Glimpses of Architecture in Kerala

Temples and Palaces

Ramu Katakam

Photographs by
Joginder Singh

Rupa & Co

It is important to warn the reader that in Kerala non-Hindus are rarely allowed to visit the temples. Photography inside is strictly prohibited and special permissions have been obtained in order to illustrate some aspects of the wonderful forms of Kerala temples. Unlike other parts of India, taking a picture of the idol is not permitted at all. Some of the idols are masterpieces of art especially the Vishnu image at Vallabha temple, Thiruvalla, which is stunningly beautiful when lit with lamps. Many of the Siva images are almost abstract in nature and have a great presence. The extraordinary strictness of ritual has kept most of the temples in pristine condition and the only noise permitted is when musical instruments are used to accompany the idol when it is taken around the temple. The intensity that is maintained, of keeping the old order, is surprising in today's fast changing world.

CONTENTS

INTRODUCTION

The clarity and simplicity of the timber architecture of Kerala has always attracted me to visiting this part of India on many occasions. When a colleague asked me to write about a particular building that had affected me more than others, I took the matter of looking at Kerala architecture more closely. I have reproduced the article as the starting point of this book because the words seem to capture the essence of the images that follow.

Across all things move the soul
And unique space:
The inner space of the world, silently
fly the birds wholly through us
Oh, I who wish to grow, I
Look without and it is in me
That the tree grows
Rilke

As you age you become conscious of the persistent and life-long movement of individuals on this planet. The planet itself is moving in several directions, and simultaneously, an individual generates further vectors of action. A force that appears to be churning almost like the perpetual churning of the oceans. In this world of movement, the mind tries to find a place of repose.

Architecture, in my view, is a microcosm of one's own mind. On entering a room, what appears to be perfect at one moment rapidly changes as one walks through it. As I grew to assimilate some of the great buildings, many changes occurred in my view of them. In the early part of my career, I saw Fathepur Sikri as the perfect composition. The royal courtyard at that time was the right blend of detail, planning and design. It captured a balance between Hindu motifs and Moghul decoration, reflecting the secular nature of Akbar's thinking. That was what good architecture was about.

But as the years went by, different places gave more fulfillment. Getting off the train at Jaisalmer early one morning, I got a view of the fort lit up by the rising sun; it appeared to be made of gold. On a visit to the Greek Island of Santorini, I saw its white dwellings atop a volcano against the backdrop of the Mediterranean. Each place left a distilled image in the mind; each confrontation with a place created a hunger for more. The ruins at Hampi, the Forbidden City in Beijing, the cliff dwellings of Mesa Verde and the temples of Luxor. And yet the hunger persisted.

It was only on a visit to Elephanta caves near Mumbai that I received my first awakening to another kind of architecture. For the first time, architecture gave me a clue that I had to keep still. It was with this stillness that a glimmer of the world beyond is perceived. The changed view of architecture touched the very basis of my perception. It was Siva at Elephanta who made me stop and stand still.

And I remembered what father Favel Florensky, the Russian philosopher and historian wrote: 'For within ourselves life in the visible world alternates with life in the invisible world and thus we experience moments – sometimes brief, sometimes extraordinarily fleeting, sometimes even the tiniest atom of time – when the two worlds grow so near in us that we can see their intimate touching. At such moments, the veil of visibility is torn apart and through that tear – that break, we are conscious of that moment – we sense the invisible world is breathing and both this and the other world are dissolving into each other. Our life at such moments becomes an unceasing stream in the same way that air when warmed streams upward from the heart.'

The moment I entered the Ettamannur temple in Kerala, I was seized with the awareness Florensky described. There are clearly two worlds coexisting in this temple – the experience of pure space and the moment of complete freedom. When that realization dawned, I knew the search was over; the hunger for yet more architecture had been driven away.

At first of course, the professional architect in me had to examine the design, the plan and materials. The simplicity of the layout, the structure's attention to detail. What came to mind then, was a Japanese temple, and the term for this kind of planning called 'Ma' or place making. An attempt to find order in disorder. As if one of many scattered beans on a polished floor holds the balance of the whole composition. In Kerala the grouping of structures within a rectangular court follows the same idea. Local materials are put together with tenderness and care, and nothing appears out of place. Such architecture has maintained a continuity over the past 900 years, and over the period, changed little in design. But like individuals, each temple is unique.

To me, Ettamannur is a place of peace that gave me an opportunity to glimpse the invisible world. A world inside myself. Within its stillness the temple promised me many memorable moments. One of them was the time of prayer, when crowds milled about, and the fragrance of jasmine hung in the air. Among the abundance of colour and lovely faces, chaos reigned – and I was completely overwhelmed by the flow.

Close to the temple, emerald-coloured rice fields and the golden light of the setting sun gave me a reassurance of purpose. By late evening, a quiet descended as I walked around the courtyard; the outside world was forgotten and left behind. The solitude among the buildings and the spaces between them left me little to ask for. As daylight receded, the oil lamps were lit and the space enveloped me yet again. The wall of the temple lit by thousands of lamps was a great wall of light dissolving the solidity of the daytime into an illusion: the illusion perhaps of existence.

As I turned to walk out of the rear, towards the trees and vegetation, the mind emptied itself and stillness enveloped me. A wild champa growing against the outer wall released its fragrance and once again it felt as if everything had stopped moving.

The Sri Subramanyaswami
temple situated
in Kochu Ollur,
Thiruvananthapuram is
the focus of worship
in that area.

12 NATURE OF THE UNIVERSE

RAMA: "When there are countless universes rising and dissolving in the infinite conciousness, why do you teach me of their nature?"

SAGE VASHISTA: "In that way you have gained the understanding that the world is a long dream. You have gained knowledge of the relationship between a world and its meaning or the objects it denotes. Hence all this discussion of the world – appearance and imaginary creation has not been in vain... when, having known all that there is to be known. You attain knowledge of the three periods of time (past, present and future), you will see all this to be true. In every atom of existence there are countless universes – who has the power to even count them?"

This view of nearly 10,000 galaxies is the deepest portrait of the visible universe available. Taken in March 2004 by the hubble telescope, the galaxy studded view represents a sample of the universe that cuts across billions of light years. According to NASA these galaxies chronicle a period when the universe was younger, more chaotic and when order and structure were beginning to emerge.

14 ARCHITECTURE IN KERALA

Temples are part of the people of Kerala. Their lives are related to them, not just in prayer, but in dance and the arts, so the temple becomes the focus of people's lives. In trying to examine places of worship, it is simple to look at their architectural merits but as one looks deeper, the spaces inside take on another dimension. It is as if one comes alive again. The intense activities of festivals, plays, discussion and prayer that take place overwhelm the visitor and when the temple is empty and silent, it gives a sense of peace and a view of the eternal.

A Kerala temple is usually low in profile and set in a beautiful part of the countryside. Traditionally the building height was not allowed to be higher than a coconut tree as it was intended that devotees should not be in awe of the building. Among the temples that break this rule are Peruvanam and Vadakunnatha at Thrissur. Dedicated to Siva, both have a monumental quality and are exceptionally exciting to visit.

It is the intent of this book to experience a glimpse of the wonderful traditional buildings of Kerala. Padmanabhapuram palace has been photographed often but cannot be excluded from any book on traditional Kerala architecture. Images of the major temples are the main focus but the quality of domestic timber structures find a place in the book. The intimate homes made completely in wood are a unique part of the state's heritage and are now being restored and looked after by many families.

Proportion, geometry and simplicity are the features that make traditional Kerala architecture eventful. In turn, the buildings look to light and space to confirm their presence. In a country that has used stone to create art and architecture, Kerala has used wood. Tamil Nadu that neighbours Kerala has developed an extraordinary legend of art, from the Hindu myths carved out at Mahabalipuram to the grandeur of Bridheshvara temple at Tanjore.

The designers and sculptors of Tamil Nadu have been able to illustrate their immense offerings for many centuries. In Kerala, however, building and art appear to have evolved completely differently. It is not easy to understand why this part of the subcontinent stands alone in its approach to design and building construction. Before the revival of Hindu thought about 1300 years ago, Buddhists and the Jain faith flourished for more than a millennium. The impact on art and architecture was enormous until the return of Hinduism as the main faith.

Kerala's natural reserve of forests provided ample wood to build timber structures that were to dominate methods of construction for a long period. The base of the structure from foundation to plinth was made of stone and then wood was used to make the walls and roof structure. Before the moulded tile appeared in India, the common rounded pottery tile was used but with the use of circular roofs copper tiles had to be introduced – partly because they could be shaped to suit the circular roof and partly because of their capability to weather the strong rains. Copper can be seen to provide a more aesthetic surface as it changes colour with age.

The evolution of the simple plan and shapes was from the early dwelling that, over a period of time, got refined in detail and scale. They did however, follow a careful set of measurements that have been laid out in an ancient building code of Kerala. Units of measurements are related to parts of the human body – one of the major ones being the distance between the top of the middle finger to the tip of the elbow. Much before Corbusier in the modern era evolved a proportion for building based on the human scale, one sees buildings being made based on the human body to create a form that is in balance with man. The slope of the roofs are usually constant even though the size and plan shapes are different. This seems to create a pleasing line for the eye. Many of the roofs of modern buildings seem to be distorted and out of proportion, jarring the eye.

Palaces and wooden houses also followed the policy of keeping the slopes at a uniform angle – the main reason for the array of roofs at

Padmanabhapuram remaining balanced and in perfect harmony. More important is that the roof form creates different compositions and is able to interact visually with the sky and surrounding landscape. In the pages that follow, the reader will be struck by this aspect being the single most important feature that brings together the superb quality of design and workmanship in the architecture.

The availability of a large quantity of timber, including varieties of rosewood, made its use extensive. A timber, known locally as Anjali, is very strong and used for the main rafters whereas wood from the Jackfruit tree was more commonly used for doors and chests for storage. The easy workability of wood allowed for the intricate design elements that appear in the beams and rafters. Later murals in wood became part of the decoration apart from the myths that were portrayed. The Kaviyur temple that is extensively described later in the book is perhaps the finest example of an early temple where wood carving had reached a peak in development. The intricacy and detail to which the sculptors were willing to experiment with is seen clearly and if one had to choose just one temple to visit in Kerala, Kaviyur would certainly be the place to go.

Granite was used extensively for foundation and plinth. Floors were also largely made of this hard stone. The section of the plinth design evolved over the years. In H. Sarkar's book, the different types of plinths are explained in depth and it is from these sections that he is able to date the temples. One aspect of the floor layout is that the stone is always placed in a random fashion – there is never a fixed pattern and this is one feature that Kerala temples share with other temples around the country. Even with the highest form of design such as those found in Khajuraho (built a thousand years ago) the floor patterns are laid out at random. In the inner court of the Kerala temple there is usually a set of markers that devotees need to follow to go around the Srikovil (the main shrine). In Siva temples the devotee has to turn back at the point where the overflow carrying excess water from the garbha-griha (space enclosing the idol) flows. The markings on this route are a set of stone pieces known as bali-peethas. A diagram of these bali-peethas appears later – they represent the positions of Devas (gods of the Hindu pantheon) in relation to the main idol.

Laterite stone is common in the northern part of the state and is used extensively as the main building material. Lime mortar and plaster were also used with laterite to make the foundations, plinths and walls of the northern temples. Many of the walls made in this way were later painted with murals depicting scenes of the myths connected to the idol worshipped in that particular temple.

Copper tiles cover the roofs and play an important role in expressing the architecture of Kerala. The small tile when seen in an expanse of roofs in all shapes and sizes, forms beautiful silhouettes enhancing the geometry of these structures. The varying hues of copper due to ageing and weathering appear to improve the roof form in every instance. It is the use of three materials – copper, timber and stone that combine to create these masterpieces of form and space.

Two areas in the subcontinent also have temples made in wood. One is Nepal and the other Himachal Pradesh near the Himalayas. The design and architecture of the temples in these places is also magnificent. The scholar Ronald Bernier has studied both the temples of Kerala and those of the Himalayas in his books *Splendours of Kerala* and *Wooden Temples of the Western Himalayas* but does not link the two styles in any way. The source of design of the two areas has clearly evolved separately.

Many have tried to compare Japanese wooden temples with the ones in Kerala but it is clear there is no connection. The structures follow similar design technology such as the trusses and rafters but here the similarity ends. The details of construction are completely different and proportion follows different norms. Perhaps Parasurama, when creating Kerala, was helped by the master craftsman Vishvakarma to evolve the style of these temples that in many ways seem to have had divine intervention in their construction. Today this land is being torn apart with huge buildings that have little aesthetic appeal.

The roofs are made of concrete and have no harmony. Fortunately the temples have been looked after very well and this will continue, as long as there is a tradition of prayer and ritual.

Guruvayur and Sabrimala temples are the two most important places of pilgrimage in Kerala. They attract hundreds of thousands of pilgrims every year. The power of these places is supposed to be immense and difficult to describe but they do not find a place in this book, as permissions for photography were difficult to obtain. They represent to the devotees complete faith in the god they are worshipping whereas the smaller shrines also form a focus to people's lives and become part of their daily routine.

It is also interesting to note that temples are not just places of worship but also places to stay and cater to all the needs of a large home with a well-equipped kitchen and an abundant water supply from the well that is situated in the outer quadrangle. Most temples have bathing tanks close by and some have large water bodies. These are not used so often today for their original purpose but still are very much part of the temple's life.

In this book, the writer has concentrated on the form of the temple and the decoration that goes with it and images of water and sky interacting with the form of the buildings. Sometimes it is possible to capture the spirit of the place, but for the pilgrims and devotees it is mainly the salvation or blessing from the god they are praying for. One is always amazed at the intense conviction of devotees and their complete faith in the protection provided by Vishnu or Siva.

The only time I felt the need to stay near an idol was at the Sri Vallabha temple in Thiruvalla when the silver image of Vishnu was lit up with one or two lamps. The stillness of the flame and the stillness seen in Vishnu was really a discovery of a stillness within. It was this event that made me travel to all parts of Kerala trying to experience this again. Although the temples have always provided a strong presence and some like Anantha Padmanabhaswami great visual delight, the Vallabha shrine has given the most peace. Form, space and light are just the beginnings of a search. The beautiful lamps, lovely flowers on womens' hair and the darkness of the garbha-griha are just hints at finding an answer to the greater truths.

Kaviyur is a temple that has extraordinary presence. It is set on elevated ground and one has to climb a number of steps to enter the inner court. The inner court early in the morning is a magical experience. The temple is small and the intimacy of spaces makes one feel part of it. It is a masterpiece of design with views of the countryside all around. It is an ancient temple and the form kept as close to the original as is possible.

For the scholar there are a number of sources to follow up as the Kerala temple has been extensively studied. The select bibliography has enough leads to pursue this subject further. It is worth mentioning that H. Sarkar's path breaking work for the Archaeological Survey *Temples of Kerala* is of prime importance. S. Jayashankar's monumental work in cataloguing the rituals and details of all the Kerala temples (there are close to 20,000) is a labour of love and dedication. Jayashankar is a rare scholar who has been photographing and describing every temple. So far he has covered five districts. He is hoping he will live long enough to complete the task. In this review, the attempt is to present the architecture and capture the essence of each building. In this quest some magnificent timber sculpture and murals were discovered and have been included.

The Dalai Lama has commented that in an age of rapid change, there is a risk of ignoring the tried and tested. The Kerala temple does not deviate from following this tradition. There are 900 years of history and continuity to these temples and many may have even more antique beginnings. It is said that some of the lamps' flames have been kept alive for over 300 years. Prayer and devotion for so long are bound to create places of intense spiritual force. These hidden treasures need to be discovered, although in doing this, they may lose their secluded quality and special relationship to the community they serve.

22 SRI MAHADEVA TEMPLE
Ettumanoor

Ettumanoor is among the best known temples of Kerala. It is an architectural masterpiece with its perfectly proportioned buildings and simplicity of form resulting in an exceptional quality of space.

As one becomes aware of the space, one is confronted with wooden carvings of intense intricacy and detail. The carvings tell the stories of the myths and legends of Hindu gods. As soon as one enters Ettumanoor, one is seized with a world of pure space and a sense of freedom. Even with the immense crowds that throng the place, moments of stillness are apparent. These moments of joy are heightened by the abundance of colour and lovely faces among the devotees. Many fragrances fill the air and the flow of people appears to envelop the visitor.

By late evening quietness descends as one goes around the courtyard and the outside world is left behind. The solitude of being with these buildings and spaces leaves you with a sense of completeness. With daylight receding, the oil lamps get lit and the dying light of the sky allows one to get a glimpse of the 'infinite'.

Close to the temple are emerald coloured rice fields lit up by the setting sun. The golden reflections on the water and the vast expanses of green give one a measure of the abundant generosity of nature. The shades of green throughout the countryside always seem to surprise the eye.

Ettumanoor is a temple devoted to Siva and is believed to have been renovated to its present form in the late 16th century AD. There is evidence that the first structures were built in the 12th century.

The temple
exterior with a lamp
in the foreground.

Ettumanoor temple seen from the rear. Each square in the wooden framework has one or two lamps which are lit on special occasions resulting in a wall of dancing flames.

26 VADAKKUNNATHA SIVA TEMPLE
Thrissur

Vadakkunnatha is perhaps the largest and best-known temple in Kerala. One of the reasons for its fame is the Pooram festival celebrated here. A spectacular event consisting of a competition between two city temples presenting the idols of goddess Devi to Siva. The larger the number of elephants used and more pomp the better. Drums and music are brought to a frenzied climax as parasols are displayed on elephants lined up on either side. Part of the celebration is to judge which temple is able to decorate the parasols and elephants better. Crowds throng the maidan or park where this celebration takes place. A magnificent display of fireworks held in the evening brings the festival to a climax.

Set in the heart of the city, Vadakkunnatha is a triple-shrined temple. The main shrine dedicated to Mahadeva (Siva) is circular and on the north side of the inner court. The temple is believed to have originated in the 9th century but evidence from inscriptions confirms its existence from the 11th century. A vast area of land encompasses the temple complex forming the only vacant space in a fast growing city.

Situated in the outer quadrangle is one of the finest Koothambalams (a large hall for theatre and dance performances) in Kerala. The timber structure is awe inspiring in scale and quality of woodwork. Inside the building are activities like the narration of scriptures where the storyteller is dressed dramatically and is accompanied by drums and music. These performances are usually in the evenings while some mornings, priests-in-residence discuss philosophy and beliefs with devotees. The outer quadrangle becomes a space for all other activities after the prayers are offered within the inner court.

A close up of the turmeric
coated nagas within the
Vadakkunnatha temple
in the outer court.
Bright sunshine falling on
them makes them almost
come alive.

Vadakkunnatha
photographed from a
distance, surrounded by
trees. The Pooram festival
was created to appease
the gods when a ruler in
the 17th century had cut
down a dense forest
around the temple.

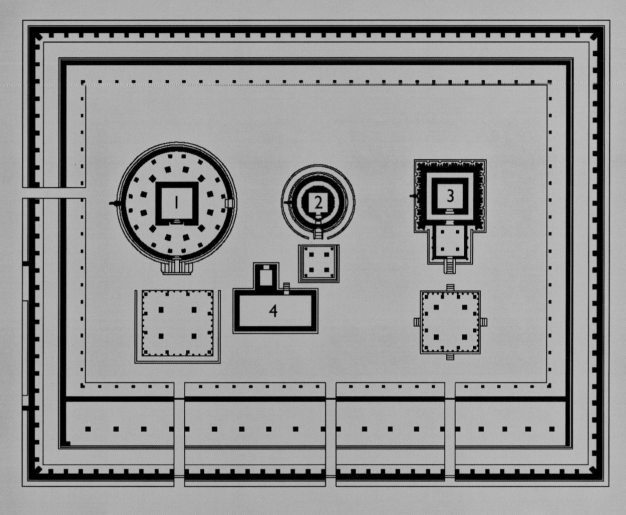

N

1. Vadakkunnatha shrine
2. Sankaranarayana shrine
3. Rama shrine
4. Ganapathy shrine

Goddess coated with
turmeric in the outer
court at Vadakkunnatha.

Detailed view of the
brackets inside the
Koothambalam stage.

Some of the images captured in these pages do convey the atmosphere that the temple has but it is difficult to convey the fervour of the devotees on Sivratri night (the darkest night of the year that is dedicated to Siva). One unique feature of the Siva shrine is the mountain of ghee that covers the lingam. Ghee (clarified butter) is poured on the idol as the main offering for prayer. It does not melt and adheres to the existing layers even though temperatures reach well above its melting point. The huge mass of ghee sometimes gets broken when the fireworks are particularly loud.

Vadakkunnatha, like most other temples in Kerala is an oasis in the centre of Thrissur. It is possible to spend the whole day there and come away refreshed.

A silk cotton tree flowering next to the southern gateway of the Vadakkunnatha temple, Thrissur.

left The shrine of Rama within the Vadakkunnatha inner court.

left below Detail of a brass bali-peetha in the courtyard.

right Bulls made of cloth and straw on a timber structure at the Vishu festival that celebrates the Kerala new year.

left Elephants waiting to
join the festivities,
wearing the finest
decorations.

left below
Decorated parasols
carried on top of
the elephants.

right Musicians at the
Pooram festival, Thrissur.

overleaf Vadakkunnatha
lit up during Sivaratri.

left The magnificent laterite wall that surrounds the temple. This design is often seen in other parts of the state.

right Vadakkunnatha's Koothambalam (temple theatre) is probably the best known in India. Built in the 17th century, it is the newest building on the campus. It offers a possibility of achieving perfect proportions for a building although the roof form is so imposing.

left Interior view of
the Koothambalam
showing the stage and
awe inspiring elements
of the roof structure.

right Corner detail
of the stage roof.

left A view of the Koothambalam from the outer court.

right Columns and rafters that show the quality of workmanship and attention to detail.

SRI MAHADEVA TEMPLE
Peruvanam

Peruvanam temple is situated about 10 km south of Thrissur
and is likely to have been built close to the time Vadakkunnatha was
established. This is where the similarity ends – Peruvanam is an
architectural masterpiece. Someone decided to bend the rules related
to keeping the height limited and built a larger structure for one of
the shrines and kept the circular srikovil (main shrine) traditionally
low. The result: one is able to see the entire temple, which is difficult
in other places. The outer court is a huge expanse of space giving
enough distance to separate it from the chaos on the main road.
On entering the court the change in pace is immediate and one
becomes aware of the sense of quiet within the temple premises.

A major street on the east side leading up to the temple is a
powerful axis with smaller lanes connecting to it. The street was
originally a connection to the neighbouring village but with houses
coming up on both sides it has become a perfect example of how
a settlement should grow. During the morning prayers, children are
found using the outer court as a short cut to school. Some stop to
offer prayers while others stop their chattering while traversing the
court. For the rest of the day the space remains a quiet haven for
visitors disturbed only by the odd cow or goat.

The circular srikovil has two lingams in the garbha-griha
(sanctuary of the idol) – a very rare occurence in a temple devoted
to Siva. The other shrine on a higher level has the image of
Umamaheswari and Siva. It is the beautiful painted sculptures
along with the murals in similar colours that surround the srikovil
which give a special feel to the inner court.

An idol of Nageshwara
(the snake god) coated
with turmeric in the
Varkala temple complex,
stands among the array
of snake idols below a
majestic banyan tree.

Peruvanam is a monumental
temple unlike other places of
worship yet it maintains the
scale and proportion that
allows a quietness found
within the court.

Intricately painted
sculptures surround
the Srikovil at
Peruvanam.
The images
captured here show
the atmosphere of
the inner court.

left Ganesh makes a rare appearance in one of the wooden columns of the Namaskara mandapa.

right Close up of the larger shrine. Devotees going around the court wall give an idea of the scale of the building.

left The street leading to Peruvanam temple from the east leads to the bathing tank and rice fields beyond. Houses are built on both sides illustrating a perfect example of how it is possible to live with nature yet have a settlement that is centred around a major temple.

55

Chapels and shrines in the Kerala countryside are not countable. They appear in every little corner and seem to capture the focus of a settlement. One particular shrine close to Kottayam belongs to a family with an Ayurvedic tradition. The Ayurvedic knowledge of Kerala has been given by the sages to eight families. This family is one of them and have looked after the shrine for over 300 years. The present physician and head of the family has tried to keep the shrine in good condition but admitted that in the past the family had much more resources and the temple was kept in a pristine state. In an earlier era they were able to feed and support many Brahmins, as was the custom at the time. Today the dining areas do not exist although the platforms where they stood are visible. The bathing tank close by is in good order and the shrine is still cared for.

The intimacy and scale of a family temple is enjoyable to experience. On those occasions when the wall lamps are lit, the shrine has a magical quality. In many ways they are as spiritually lifting as the major temples. Many of these small shrines are empty and the silence and solitude are magnified as one wanders through the outer court. It is also important to note that prayers are whispered to the gods, enhancing the atmosphere of silence.

A shrine in the Peruvanam area set in the fields.

Sri Anantha Padmanabhaswami Temple, Thiruvananthapuram

This temple in Thiruvananthapuram is dedicated to Anantha Padmanabhaswami. It became the reason for Maharaja Marthanda Varma to move from his old capital of Padmanabhapuram. The ruler undertook to give his kingdom to the god Padmanabhaswami and promised to look after it for him. Unlike other Kerala temples, a gopuram or gateway to the temple was built in the style of the Tamil Nadu temples.

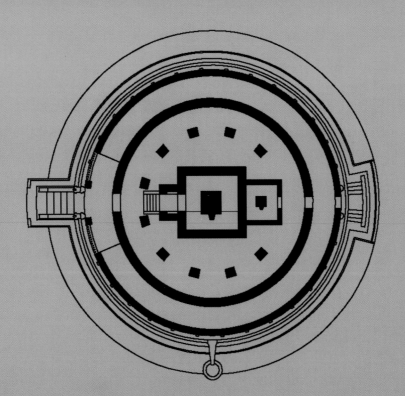

SRI VALLABHASWAMI TEMPLE
Thiruvalla

The Sri Vallabha temple at Thiruvalla near Kottayam in central Kerala is one of the classics of temple architecture. Ronald Bernier, in his treatise on Kerala temples comments, "its sculpture of stone and wood are among the finest in Kerala." The idol belonging to this temple is a magnificent rendering of Vishnu and has been made by a master craftsman. Legends proclaim that it was made by Vishvakarma (lord of the craftsmen) himself. Manuscripts suggest a very early date for the temple's consecration and hence its fame as a Vishnu temple. Constant repair and restoration of the wooden temples make it difficult to date this temple but the original idol probably goes back to the 1st century BC.

Apart from the major Hindu festivals, temples celebrate their own special festival once a year. Celebrations can go on for a week during which dance and drama performances take place in the evenings. It is a time for people living around this area to gather and meet and an occasion for individuals to return to their homes, if they live far away, to spend a few days with family and friends. During the festivities the lamps on the walls are lit every evening. Thousands of lamps that have been filled with oil and wicks come alive as devotees scramble to light them. The transformation takes a few minutes, leaving the visitor marvelling at the new image of the temple as a blaze of light.

On the occasion when the picture overleaf was captured, the gods rewarded the photographer with a thundershower, leaving the area full of water. The illusion of the temple floating on water made one feel that in all these months, even if we came away with this one image the whole project would have been worthwhile.

The timber structure lit up with lamps inside and outside again reinforces the strength of wooden architecture. The size and scale of each space seem to be in perfect harmony with the other.

left Entrance to the Sri Vallabha temple.

overleaf
Sri Vallabha temple.
As darkness surrounds the temple, the lamps on the walls are lit which turns the wall into a screen of dancing flames. To the visitor it appears to reflect the illusion of life where one is not sure whether a wall exists or is a composition of floating oil lamps.

The interior of the
entrance of Sri Vallabha,
lit up for a special
occasion.

Moss growing over a
temple wall.

Sri Subramanyaswami Temple, Haripad

Side elevation of the Koothambalam at Haripad. This version of a temple theatre is well known and is much older than the one at Thrissur.

Koothambalam, Haripad.
The scale of the roof
enhances the space
dramatically and the
woodwork appears to
be perfectly designed.

Interior of the
Koothambalam, Haripad.

Detail showing the workmanship on the beams. Note the lizard that the carver could not resist adding.
The painter, more recently, was then tempted to highlight this feature.

Detail of the woodwork
seen from inside the gable
in the Koothambalam.
Bringing in light and at the
same time controlling glare
are major features of these
theatres.

SRI PARASURAMASWAMI TEMPLE
Thiruvallam

Situated close to Thiruvananthapuram at Thiruvallam, the Parasuramaswami temple could be among the early temples of Kerala. Named after Parasurama, the god who created Kerala, it has the unique feature of having more than one god being worshipped at the temple. Within the inner court, there exist shrines of Mahadeva (Siva), Parasurama, Brahma and Mathya murthi. The earliest is said to have been built in the 13th century while the Siva shrine is dated to the 17th century.

A shrine for Brahma is generally rare in Kerala which makes this temple even more different from the others. It is perhaps the only one to have a reincarnation of Vishnu, Brahma and Siva together forming the triumvirate that creates the universe. Although the shrines have been built over a four-century period, the balance between the architectural styles and space seem to have been maintained. The inner court has a blend of human scale and intimacy. Seen in the early morning light, the temple suggests a sense of serenity and calm. The tall brass tower does not appear to be in the conventional spot but outside the temple. It also has, on the top, a beautifully carved Nandi (sitting bull).

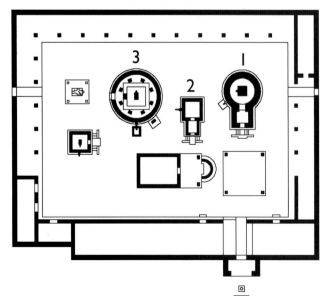

1. Parasurama shrine
2. Brahma shrine
3. Siva shrine

76

Parasuramaswami at
daybreak.

78

View of the inner
court showing the
different shrines in this
temple. The intimacy of
space between them
makes for a good
visual balance.

Detail of stone and stucco
on the roof of a shrine
shows the influence of
design from Tamil Nadu.

Wood from the jackfruit tree has a rich colour when freshly cut. It is commonly used for chests and doors.

82 The following pages have examples
of interiors showing the design and
workmanship of the timber structure.
The light quality in each image
varies but illustrates the attention
paid to illuminating a space.

Detail of the rafters in an
open pavilion.

Detail of the rafters
in a more closed space
where the quality of light
is subdued yet makes the
space come alive.

The roof at the Padmanabhapuram dining hall. Large spans have been made with a simple design, exhibiting a robustness in the structure.

86 SRI MAHADEVA TEMPLE
Vazhapalli

Vazhapalli is situated close to Kottayam. The wood carvings are intense as at Kaviyur but have been spoilt by varnishing of the images. The inner court of the temple is seen on the facing page

Women praying at a small open shrine in the outer court of Vazhapalli gives one the conviction that there is a god that looks after them.

KRISHNAPURAM PALACE
near Kayankulam

89

Built close to Kayankulam in south Kerala, this palace was the residence of a raja of a smaller kingdom. It is a very good example of a secular building made in timber that has survived. Now a museum, many beautiful sculptures of nagas (snakes) are exhibited. In the neighbourhood is the famous Mannarshala – a grove full of trees that have existed well before the temples. The grove is full of serpents that are worshipped and looked after. A small temple has been built nearby that attracts thousands of devotees.

Krishnapuram palace has a beautiful architectural quality and the large water body gives it balance. From its large compound, one does not realise the main road is a few meters away. As one walks through the building, it is clear the rulers of the past lived austere lives and did away with the pomp and extravagance that is seen in other parts of India.

A temple umbrella made of palm leaves and bamboo is put away in a quiet corner of a temple.

Krishnapuram palace seen
from the west.

The stone sculpture
of a Nageshwara is part of
the museum collection
at Krishnapuram.
The entwining cobras at
the back are unique and
make it a wonderful work
of art.

Detail of the first floor balcony seen from the inside gives the visitor an idea of how the glare was cut down without compromising on the light and breeze.

An external view of the
same space illustrating
the quality and detail of
timber used.

The quality and
proportion of this
building that keeps to
the traditional methods
of construction and design
gives us an example of
great architecture.

SRI MAHADEVA TEMPLE
Vaikom

Vaikom is a major pilgrimage center and it represents a peak of
temple architecture in Kerala in the same way as Ettumanoor temple
situated close by. Dated to the 17th century in its present form (both
Ettumanoor and Vaikom have much earlier beginnings), the design style
manages to achieve a perfect balance with the countryside. The use
of copper tiles to cover the roofs to create their round shapes
contributes to the beauty of these simple forms.

   Dedicated to Mahadeva (Siva), the temple festival is held during
November each year when events can last upto a week. Devotees
come in large numbers to witness the festivities that include dance
and drama. Among the main rituals of the festival are firecrackers and
music accompanying the parade of the temple idol on top of richly
decorated elephants that go around the court several times.
This memorable event leaves the visitor elated, sometimes
feeling he has entered a world of fantasy.

overleaf

Vaikom seen on
a wet day.

above Roof of the
Srikovil at Vaikom.

right A bird's eye view of
one of the many shrines
that dot the countryside.
This one just behind the
Kaviyur temple gives one
an idea of the simple form
that fits in with the
greenery and water
of Kerala.

A brass Nandi close to
the lit up wall at the
Vaikom temple.
Huge crowds come
to enjoy the evening
events at the temple's
yearly festival.

Wall lamp detail.

104 WOODEN HOUSES

Kerala's wooden houses have been in existence for as long as the temples. The abundance of timber allowed the evolution of this form of construction. Larger homes are known as Illams, with rooms surrounding one or two courtyards. Occasionally the size can be extended to four courtyards.

There is usually a verandah before the main entrance. When the system of caste was more prevalent, most visitors were not allowed inside the house and this space was meant for meeting them. The first part of the house consists of a court and open areas with one or two closed rooms. The Ara or store for valuables, including rice, is located at the centre of one side of the court along the corridor and doubles as a strong room of the house with elaborate locks on it. Made entirely of wood, it is difficult to open or break into. In many of the homes the idol for worship is placed in the Ara and prayers are offered within the court.

Walls are of 'post and beam' construction while decorative rafters make up the roof. Columns are used in the open areas to support the roof beams. The cooking area is usually made of stone with the roof made in wood and tile. Strict proportions, according to the rules laid down in the building Shastras, are followed closely. These include giving the roof the correct slope in order to achieve a good proportion. Houses, like the temples, seem to achieve a form that is pleasing to the eye and fit in with the landscape.

Measurements are linked to parts of the body - a method used in many civilisations. The distance between the fingertips and the elbow is one such measure. The kitchen is normally close to the well of the house while, in temples, the well is usually on the left of the entrance. Temples are in many ways like large houses where the younger priests-in-residence have to carry out the duties of cooking, cleaning and maintaining the premises.

The residence pictured here is a beautiful example of a wooden house set in the hills of Palai in the central Kerala region. Built in the Christian tradition where no courtyards are included, this house has been built with care and has incorporated the intricate details found in traditional Illams.

Among the other images that are included is one from a poet's house that has been restored. The gable and column details give an idea of the attention to detail in creating these wonderful homes that can be a delight to live in.

A beautifully built
wooden house in the
hills of the Palai region
in central Kerala.

Details of wooden panels used
to create walls of the house.
Smaller images illustrate details of
the decorative elements in the
beams and panels.

left The quality of workmanship is seen in a
restored part of an Illam
that is now being used as
a resort hotel. The picture
shows the ceiling meeting
the panels. It also gives a
view of the Ara which is a
place to store valuables
and rice. Note the bunch
of rice stalks hanging in
front of the Ara.

right The rafters at a
house in Palai form a
rhythmic pattern.

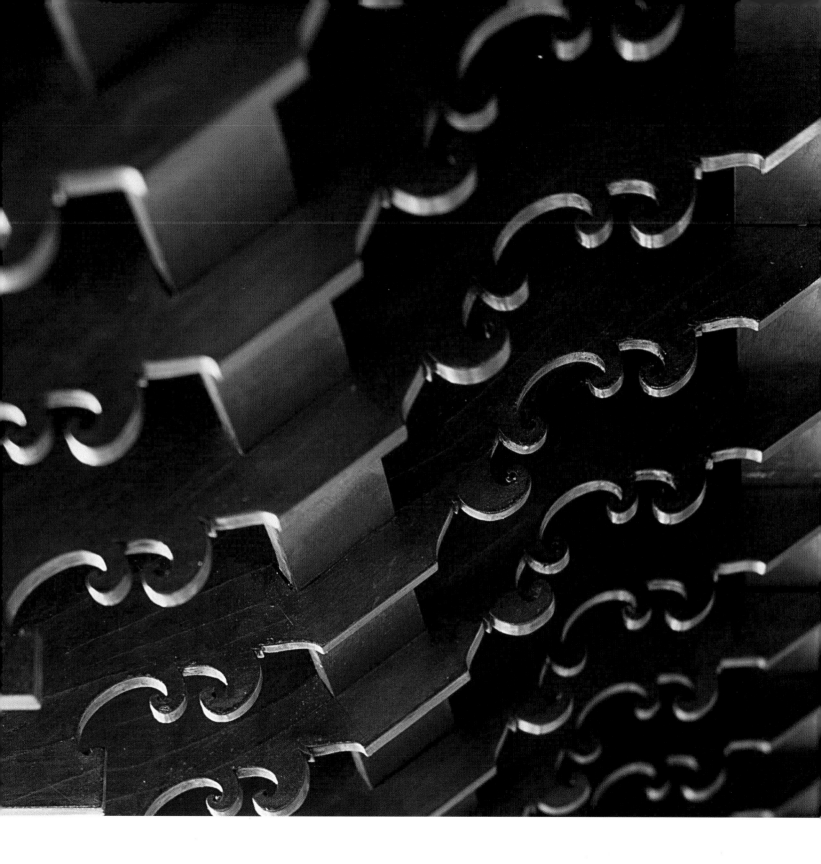

Details of the intricate
decoration seen in the
panels of wood.
The phrase 'God is in the
details' coined by Mies
van de Rohe certainly
applies here.

The designer has made a great deal of effort to see that the beam and column meeting point is as aesthetic as possible and structurally correct.

116 SRI MAHADEVA TEMPLE
Kaviyur

Kaviyur is possibly the finest temple in Kerala, from a design point of view. Situated close to Tiruvalla in central Kerala, the inscriptions on the plinth date back to well over a thousand years. The present structure is likely to be close to 500 years old and has the intimacy of what was probably intended in a typical Kerala temple. On entering the inner court, one is seized with a stillness and sense of well being. The temple has the added advantage of being built on high ground where the visitor has to climb a set of steps to the main entrance.

Dedicated to Mahadeva (Siva), it offers the devotee the chance to encapsulate the Hindu faith. Siva is the idol that is worshipped here, whereas the stories of the Ramayana and Mahabharata are told in the form of carvings that are fixed to the wall of the srikovil. The Devas or lesser Gods find a place in the circular wall usually facing the direction each has been attributed with. Indra, god of the heavens is at the head of the pantheon and is the first panel whereas Agni, the god of fire, faces south east. Each panel is separated by a column and as one goes around in a clockwise direction each alternate column has an avatar of Lord Vishnu carved on it. The other set of columns have a carving of each of the Devas. Yama, the god of death, appears facing south while Varuna, god of the west, resides in that direction. Nirudhu, the god of departed souls, faces south west. Vaayu, god of the winds, faces north west. Kubhera, lord of wealth, faces west.

In the panels, the Ramayana has been well illustrated with many images of Rama, Sita and Lakhsmana along with various poses of Hanuman, the monkey god, who helps Rama defeat Ravana. The panels portray Siva as the creator and destroyer of the universe while Vishnu is seen in his ten avatars.

Kaviyur is an architectural masterpiece and a delight to visit. It has been left intact with little alterations or restoration and represents a temple in Kerala as would have existed 500 years ago. This unique place of worship is the example of a perfect temple. Kaviyur is not only very ancient but has been a living temple for the same period as can be seen by the affection with which the local residents look after it.

We were fortunate to become friends of Kaviyur Shivarama Aiyar whose family came to settle here centuries ago. Shri Aiyar is now over eighty years old and is a retired headmaster. He spends his morning in prayer and much of his time in helping run the temple. His ancestral home is walking distance from the temple and one could see why he has chosen to remain in this small town. A man of great generosity and spirit, he was prepared to spend time explaining the stories depicted in the wooden carvings. His contribution is a book in Malayalam that explains the stories behind the carvings on the ceiling of the Namaskara mandapa. Unfortunately these wonderful specimens that contain the complete story of the Ramayana cannot be photographed with natural light. Hanuman's participation in the war with Ravana is covered extensively. I hope it will be possible for some-one to document these carvings in detail, as they may soon be lost due to lack of care.

Kaviyur should be given special status as a protected monument in the same degree as Khajuraho or Padmanabhapuram. More important than the art and architecture of Kaviyur is the sense of elation and excitement it provides. A moment when one realises it may be worth being in this universe.

left Roofscape at Kaviyur.

right Looking into the inner court at Kaviyur showing the srikovil.

left Oil being filled in the wall lamps for lighting later in the evening.

right Gable detail at entrance to Kaviyur.

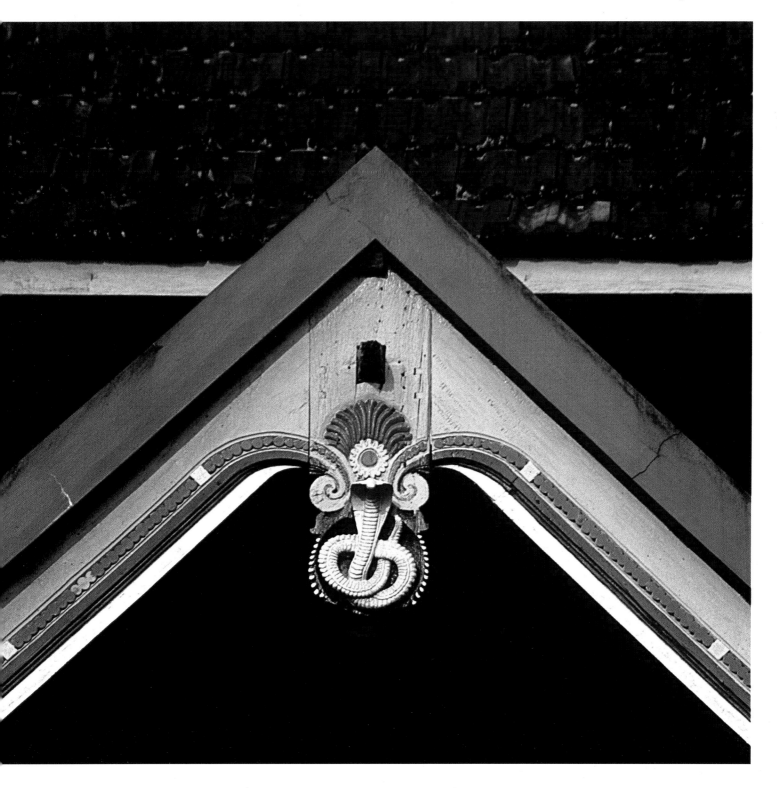

122

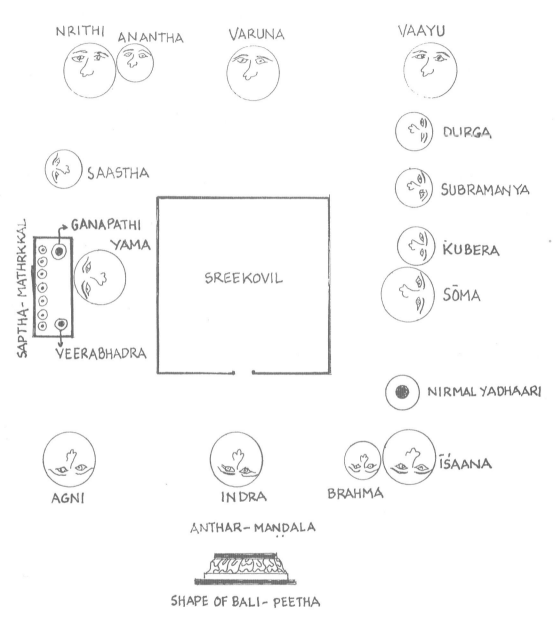

NRITHI   ANANTHA   VARUNA   VAAYU

DURGA

SAASTHA

SUBRAMANYA

GANAPATHI

YAMA

KUBERA

SAPTHA- MATHRKKAL

SREEKOVIL

SOMA

VEERABHADRA

NIRMAL YADHAARI

AGNI   INDRA   BRAHMA   ISAANA

ANTHAR- MANDALA

SHAPE OF BALI- PEETHA

POSITION OF BALI-PEETHAS IN ANTHAR-MANDALA

THE TEN AVATARS OF VISHNU

In existence there seems to be demonic forces that cause chaos. They are almost like the forces of gravity, except stronger, as they delve deep into mankind. In order to counteract these demons, Vishnu periodically visits the earth in one avatar or another. As soon as he appears as the tenth avatar, the universe is ready for destruction and starts another cycle of existence.

Starting as a giant fish Vishnu came to earth to recover the holy scriptures that had been stolen by demons and hidden deep in the ocean. The second appearance was in the form of a tortoise (kurma) when Vishnu had to help the Devas obtain the nectar of immortality. The asuras or demons were also after the nectar and churned the ocean using a giant snake (Vasuki) as the churning rope and mount Mandhera as the churning rod. To prevent the mountain from sinking into the sea the giant tortoise supported the mountain until the nectar of immortality emerged. Vishnu is said to have distributed the nectar only to the gods but this is difficult to believe, as many demons seem to have immortality today. The tortoise is a symbol of strength and stability and can be seen supporting many of the large brass lamps that are placed outside the temple. The epic of the churning of oceans appears in many sculptures in India and as far away as Java and Cambodia where the Hindu faith flourished. In Kerala however, this depiction is rarely seen.

The third avatar is in the form of a boar (Varaha). Vishnu appears in this form to retrieve Bhoomi Devi(mother earth) who has sunk to the bottom of the ocean. This theme is also often seen in Indian sculpture and rock cut panels.

In order to destroy Bali, king of the demons, Vishnu then took the form of a dwarf (Vamana). He appeared before the king while he was displaying his power and wealth at a Yagna (sacrifice) ceremony. When asked what gift he wanted, Vamana asked for three feet of land measured by his small feet. This the king immediately agreed to not realising that when Vamana took his first step it spanned the whole earth. The second step crossed all the heavens leaving no place for the third. Bali, keeping to his word, offered his head for Vamana to step on, thus vanquishing him. Another interpretation is that Parasurama did the same to the king who then ruled Kerala. The banished king was well respected and was allowed to visit for one day in the year. This is the day of Onam – Kerala's most important festival which people of all faiths celebrate with enthusiasm and fervour.

Vishnu's next incarnation as Parasurama destroyed the Kshatriyas (warriors and rulers) who had become obsessed with power. Even today there is a special pathway for the Kshatriyas in the Vadakkunnatha temple in Thrissur as they bypass Parasurama's abode in the outer court. It is Vishnu, as Parasurama, who is supposed to have created Kerala. He threw his axe into the sea and carved out a piece of land that is now known as Kerala.

Narasimha, Rama and Krishna, the next three avatars, have been described with the images in these pages. Buddha has been fondly adapted as the ninth avatar, as a man who purified Hinduism from excessive ritual. This interpretation is not used in Kaviyur where the ninth incarnation is represented as Balarama.

The last emergence of Vishnu in this cycle of the universe is Kalki. He is said to appear riding a white stallion with sword in hand to establish righteousness on earth before its destruction. Kalki is rarely portrayed but in Kaviyur he is seen as a small figure emerging from the woodwork. The legends relating to the avatars of Vishnu appear to reflect the evolution of man. From the sea to the compassion of Buddha is seen to be man's role before facing inevitable destruction.

Entrance to the Srikovil
is lit with lamps just
as the evening prayers
begin.

Last panel in the srikovil
wall with the image of
Eshwara (Siva) being
attended to by the rishis.

Detail of the base of the
stamba (tall pole in front
of all temples).

Krishna with demons
or asuras.

Matysa, the golden fish,
as Vishnu's first avatar.

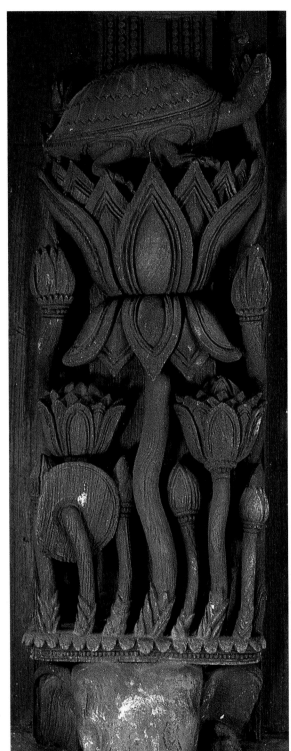

Kurma, the tortoise, who
is the base of Mount
Mandhera as it churned to
make the nectar of
immortality for the gods.

Vishnu appears as a large
boar (varaha) to retrieve
Bhoomi Devi (mother
earth) from the depths
of the sea.

Parasurama is the angry incarnation of Vishnu. He kills all the kshatriyas (warriors) who are plaguing the earth with their arrogance and power. He is the god known to have created Kerala and did this by throwing his axe in the sea and carving out a piece of land.

Agni, the god of fire, is symbolised here with his hair shown as flames.

Krishna, the eighth avatar of Vishnu.

According to the Puranas, which are a set of tales that convey the truths of the Vedas to those who cannot comprehend the texts, Vishnu came into this world in his fourth avatar as half-lion and half-man. In order to portray that god is everywhere and always comes to the help of his devotees, the story of the destruction of the demon king Hiranyakashipu is told. Prahlad is the son of the demon king but worships Vishnu. Hiranyakashipu is all powerful and instructs his son to ignore Vishnu and follow him. He tells him that man or beast cannot kill him because of the special powers he has been given nor will any weapon be able to destroy him. He also claims that he cannot die inside or outside a house nor at anytime during day or night either on earth or in the sky, making him invincible to all including the gods. To eliminate the demon Vishnu appears as Narasimha (half-man, half-lion) and kills him using his hands to tear out his insides. He does this by placing the demon king on his lap, under the arch of a doorway and choosing the twilight hour.

In this way he is neither inside nor outside, nor is it day or night. Putting him on his lap the king is neither on the earth or the sky while Narasimha is neither man or beast nor does he use any weapon and finds a way of overcoming the protection the demon king has available to him.

Narasimha destroying
the demon king
Hiranyakashipu.

Panel shows Rama as the seventh avatar of Vishnu. A monkey army surrounds him who help him defeat Ravana the evil rakshasa from Lanka.

above Lamps being
sorted.

left Entrance to Kaviyur
inner court.

The tenth and last avatar of Vishnu is still to appear. He is seen here waiting to emerge. Sword in hand and riding a white horse, Kalki will signal the end of this cycle of the universe but also bring a moment of righteousness after the horrors of the Kaliyuga we are witnessing today.

136

Draupadi had taken a vow to wash her hair in Duryodhana's blood once he was killed by Bhima. The detail of Bhima pulling out the king's intestines is an extraordinary work of art. The top panel (not featured) shows Draupadi with her hair undone and using the blood to wash her hair.

Bhima takes his revenge on Duryodhana who humiliated Draupadi by having her sari unravelled in his court. He is seen here grappling with Duryodhana who he locks in a vice like grip.

138

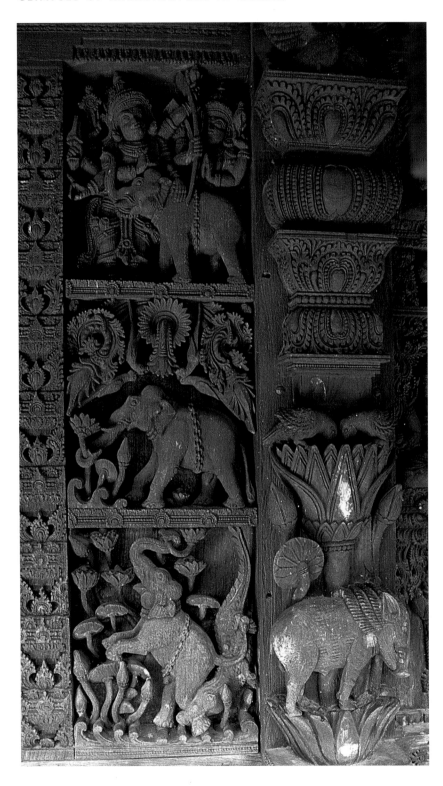

An important story depicted in the images is the devotion to Vishnu by King Indra Dhamma when he is cursed by the sage Agasthya. King Indra Dhamma is in the middle of his meditation to Vishnu when Agasthya enters his presence. Instead of recognising the sage he carries on with his prayers which makes Agasthya angry and he curses the king by turning him into an elephant and sending him to the forest. While bathing, the elephant king is trapped by an alligator (lower panel) and is pulled deep into the water. At that moment he remembers his past and offers flowers (middle panel) to Vishnu to save him. Vishnu appears and restores him to his human form and returns his kingdom to him (top panel). The event is known as the Gajendra Moksha or liberation of the elephant.

Temple elephant taking
a well deserved rest from
the festivities.

The empty inner court at Kaviyur showing a glimpse of the panels in the round wall that is the Srikovil.

Kumbhakarna seen
sleeping for six months.
He had asked the gods for
a long sleep as a boon. In
this panel, Ravana is
trying to wake him with
the help of elephants
and horses.

142

Siva seen to be killing Yama (the god of death). The image of Siva is one of rage: showing him with tusks, bow, axe and a trishul. He does this to save Markandeya from death, which is his destiny, at an early age. Markandeya appeals to Siva not to kill Yama. Siva restores Yama but as Markandeya's time of death has passed, he achieves immortality.

Early morning at the
entrance to Kaviyur.

The panel showing parts of Krishna's childhood is known as Krishna Leela, a well-known story about his exploits and his fondness for butter. On one occasion when his mother catches him stealing butter, she begins to scold him.

When Krishna starts crying, he opens his mouth to reveal the complete universe including herself. She realises that Krishna is indeed the almighty Vishnu in his eighth avatar.

Krishna is also known for his divine statesmanship in the field of battle. As the charioteer of Arjuna (the warrior prince of the Pandavas), he has the famous dialogue described in the Gita, before the beginning of the battle, between the Pandavas and the Kauravas in the Mahabharata.

Top panel shows Krishna playing the flute in the forest.

Middle panel shows Krishna opening his mouth.

Bottom panels are scenes of Krishna stealing butter and eating it.

146

above Panels depicting the coronation of Rama. Sita and some rishis are behind, blessing the event.

right Dusk at Kaviyur – a precious moment for the devotee.

left Gable detail at Kaviyur.

right View of the entrance to Kaviyur at dusk.

An image of a disused
fishing boat – the frayed
rope once held the timber
together.

152 SRI ANANTHA PADMANABHASWAMI TEMPLE, Kumbala

Anantha Padmanabhaswami temple is named after the deity Anantha Padmanabhaswami and is situated in a quiet corner of northern Kerala in Kasargod district near a place called Kumbla. Being close to south Karnataka the style of the building is a mixture of the traditional form and those found in the Coorg district close by. It has been built with laterite stone which is the main building material available. The uniqueness of this temple is that it has no outer court and is located in the middle of a fresh water lake. The lake is said to be perennial as it is fed by underground springs. In the vicinity are a number of ruins making it apparent that a major settlement existed here in the past. The picturesque location invites the visitor to stay and experience the dramatic sunsets that can be seen from this elevated site.

The temple is very isolated and has remained untouched by modern 'improvements' that usually spoil the original architecture. In this case, one is able to experience the temple as if one was going back in time. Surrounding the temple is a simple setting of rock and wild flowers giving this place a special feel and allowing the pilgrim a further chance to enhance his spirit.

Another unique feature of Anantha Padmanabhaswami is the presence of a single crocodile that has inhabited the lake since anyone can remember. The legend is that even if the crocodile dies another replaces it soon after. A British soldier visiting this area is said to have called out to the crocodile (who answers to the name of Babiya). As soon as it appeared, he shot and killed it but the soldier was bitten by a snake soon after and died . This retribution was said to have been done by the snake god Anantha. Very soon after another crocodile appeared in the lake and the villagers are convinced it is Vishnu who has left the idol and taken the form of a crocodile. The crocodile was

still there in 2002 when the writer visited the temple and clearly a mystery to all who come to Anantha Padmanabhaswami.

Sri Anantha Padmanabhaswami is the deity of Lord Vishnu reclining on the divine serpent Anantha. In this temple however, Vishnu is seen sitting on the coils of Anantha. He has the goddess of earth Bhoodevi on one side and the goddess of prosperity Sridevi on the other (a similar composition appears on the mural outside). The original idol is said to have been made from a combination of 70 different materials — an art that has long been lost. As recently as in 1998, the temple authorities were able to find an artisan from Vaikom who was the only person alive with this knowledge of creating an idol. The new set of idols resulted in the resurgence of an ancient art form.

Anantha Padmanabhaswami signifies eternal time, maintaining the phenomenon of the universe. The snake god Anantha spreads his protective hood around him while he sits in an ocean that represents eternal energy from which all phenomena emerges. Padmanabhaswami is the deity the rulers of Travancore worshipped and named their old capital Padmanbhapuram after.

It is only when Marthanda Varma, king during the 17th century, handed over his kingdom to the deity in Thiruvananthapuram, that they had to abandon the old capital and set up the new one. The ruler had promised to be a caretaker for Anantha Padmanabhaswami. Even today the Maharaja of Travancore offers prayers every morning and apprises the deity of the affairs of state.

Apart from being an exceptional piece of architecture, the temple is endowed with wonderful carvings on the ceiling of the Namskara mandapa. The vibrant murals depicting, among others, Anantha and Nataraja, complete the magical spell of this place. The glimpse inside is enchanting and represents the intent of this review on Kerala architecture.

SECTION A-A

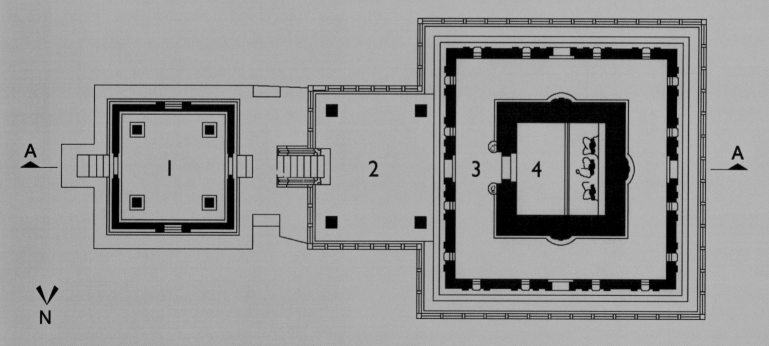

A   A

1. Namaskara mandapa (pavilion for devotion)
2. Mukha mandapa (primary pavilion)
3. Srikovil (main shrine)
4. Garbha-griha (enclosure for idol)

5   0 Meters

View of the temple from
the lakeside close to the
area where the lone
crocodile resides.

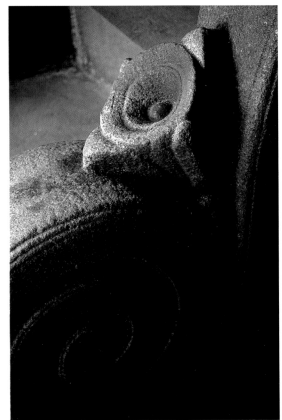

The mural depicts the idol of the temple where Vishnu is seen sitting on the serpent god Anantha. Bhoomi Devi (goddess of the earth) and Sridevi (the goddess of prosperity) are seen sitting on both sides of Vishnu.

above Devotee
at Anantha
Padmanabhaswami.

left Mural of a Nataraja
that has been partially
restored.

Frangipani in full bloom.

left Detail of an abandoned tank close by.

right Dry grass taking over a ruin.

Mural shows Vishnu
with two consorts – the
two demons at his feet
represent the forces of
chaos which even he
cannot control while
creating the universe.

An outer wall protects the murals on the wall of the garbha-griha. This picture gives a hint of the spaces in Kerala architecture. It is worth noting that this part of the temple is not normally accessible. This picture was taken during renovation work and the idol had been moved temporarily.

164

left Part of a building detail showing laterite stone work after the plaster has fallen off. This building is likely to be many centuries old.

right A temple tree set amongst the ruins.

166 SRI RAMASWAMI TEMPLE
Thiruvangad

Rama is a popular god and going to the temple, as many devotees do, early in the morning, is a joyful moment for them. Rama does not make many demands – he represents good against evil and has a sense of purpose. As one enters the Rama temple at Tiruvangaad in Tellicherri, north Kerala, there is a sense of welcome from both the devotees and the spaces inside. The inner court is full of worshippers that span all ages and walks of life. Young women, with their hair heavily oiled and gleaming, exude confidence and freshness. Older devotees are more enthusiastic whereas children appear bewildered and sometimes bored. Mothers exhibit their form of duty while young men are rigorous with the rituals yet cannot help casting a fleeting eye at the young women. A young bride seeking Rama's blessing enters dressed in white and gold, wearing a vast amount of jewellery. She looks triumphant and is a delight to the eye.

Peace prevails in the temple, yet there is also gaiety and a degree of relaxation. Siva temples on the other hand are more rigorous and austere - they seek to convey a moment of stillness within the temple and the seeker is driven to look within. Siva does find a small space on a large painting. Alongside is a beautiful rendering of Hanuman praying in a grove of banana trees – it is a fascinating interpretation of the monkey god and an exceptionally good work of art. A small shrine of Ganapathy is also located in the court while the goddess Devi finds a place in a shrine within the Namaskara mandapa.

The most significant aspect of this temple is the stunning array of wooden figures from the Ramayana. Also located in the upper reaches of the roof is a beautiful sculpture of Indra and his consort Indrani. Vishnu is depicted riding Garuda but in this instance Garuda is holding on to Vishnu's leg making it a unique composition among the exquisite sculptures. It becomes apparent that the wood carvings are the lifetime work of one devoted master sculptor. The work reflects a period when art was generated from pure devotion and prayer and the sculptor appears to have the help of the gods he is portraying. At this point one needs to ask why the creator needs a sculptor to bring about this joy while evolving the universe. It is also worth contemplating the fact that this temple was not on our list of temples to visit, yet we were drawn there just when our energy levels were beginning to sag. The renewed energy has lasted long enough to complete the book.

The prized work of carvings on the ceiling of the Namaskara mandapa was difficult to capture due to the thick layer of soot that has collected on them. This wonderful collection of friezes could compare with the best anywhere and worth seeing even if one had the time to visit only one temple. They consist of scenes from Rama's life. The southern side consists of the childhood of Rama with the appearance of sage Vishvamitra while other scenes illustrate flocks of birds and herds of elephants that come to life in the panels.

Stepping out of the temple, one was confronted by a bent old woman carrying a plastic bag full of flowers. On being given some money, which she accepted gracefully, she gave a huge toothless laugh. One could not be sure whether it was one of gratitude or one that mocked us. It left me completely unsettled and unable to absorb the excitement and art experienced a few moments earlier.

The devotees kept streaming in - our host told me he visited the temple every morning, just as the light was breaking, to offer prayers. His implicit trust in Rama in looking after his affairs has left him a content man. His generosity in terms of time and effort made me feel extremely grateful.

External view of
Rama temple.

right Garuda holding
Vishnu by the leg is
unique. The sculptor
exhibits his incredible skill
and devotion in making
this scene.

overleaf The cobras are
seen to be dancing on top
of the gable of the
entrance to the srikovil.

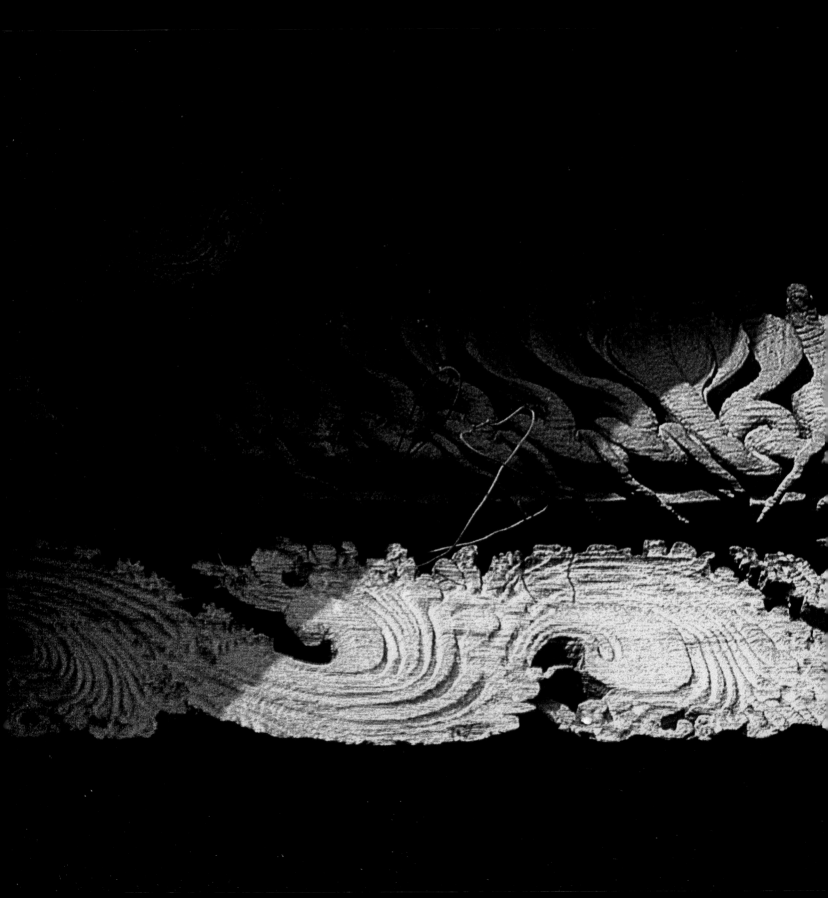

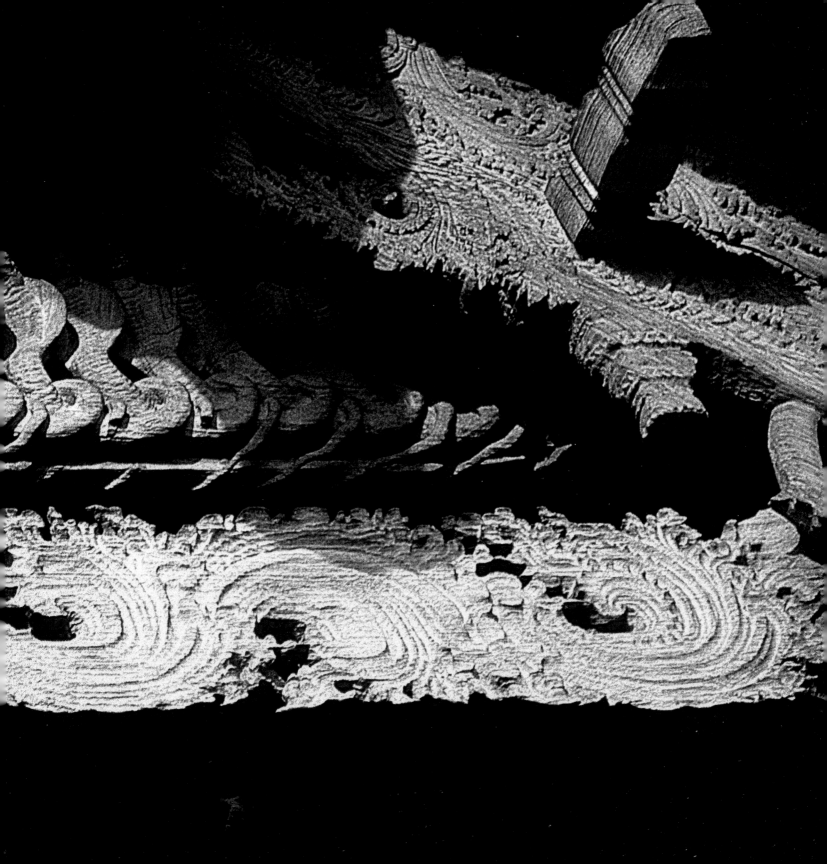

172

Rama in the blessing pose.

The eagle perched on top of the temple stamba sat there for more than three hours under the hot mid-day sun.

Two men carrying a large fish is another lifelike rendering of a Ramayana theme.

A delicately carved statue
of the god Indra and his
consort Indrani. The
massive hood of cobras
makes the sculpture special.

Carving work on the
entrance gable that stands
out among the already
intricate woodwork.

Rama and Sita.

'From the unreal lead me
to the real, from darkness
lead me to light, from
death lead me to
immortality'.

SRI MAHAVISHNU TEMPLE
Thirunelli

Visiting Thirunelli can be a tiring experience as one winds up the ghats to the higher reaches of the mountains of Wyanad. The visitor is rewarded with cool air as the taxi makes its way through the tea gardens and the coffee estates. The last 30 km is through a teak forest and towards the end one passes through magnificent bamboo groves.

The temple is perched on a small plateau and has views from all sides of the forests and hills. Dedicated to Vishnu, it appears to be much older than those close to the coast. The building is simple and the decoration minimal. The roofs are covered with copper tiles. Difficult to date, the present structure could be well over 500 years old.

It is a temple for pilgrimage and a place for final funeral rites and immersion of ashes nearby. Thirunelli's location is enviable but a little difficult to photograph. Joginder climbed up a telephone radio tower to capture the image seen on the facing page.

The Rama temple at
Thripprayar is on the
banks of a river and has an
entrance from the water
as well as the land.
Devotees are often seen
coming by boat.

Koodalmanikkam Sri Bhartharswami Temple, Irinjalakuda

Irinjalakuda's
Koothambalam is very old
and competes with the
scale and quality
of Haripad.

189

Thripoonithura is situated close to Kochi. It was an old settlement of the rajas of Kochi. The temple is surrounded by higher buildings than the other temples, which gives this complex a different grandeur.

A roof being repaired
allows a view of the rafter
design.

PADMANABHAPURAM PALACE
near Thuckalai, Tamil Nadu

Set among the hills and rocks of the southern tip of India, Padmanabhapuram is an architectural tour de force. It is unique, as a major secular building, to have survived for so long and in such good condition. It was the seat of power of the Maharajas of Travancore since the 14th century although the present structure is said to date from the 16th century. Extensively renovated by Maharaja Marthanda Varma in the 18th century, he abandoned it to live near the Padmanabhaswami temple in Thiruvanthapuram which was to become the new capital.

Like most traditional buildings in Kerala, the palace is set inside a large walled area. There are no vistas or open spaces to warn one of the presence of a major building. One enters through a large wooden gate and faces the main entrance. The entrance court allows a wonderful view of the roof set against a backdrop of hills. As one gets closer, intricate timberwork and design come into view. It is the mastery of detail and building to a human scale that sets this building apart from other palaces in India. The design is not an architectural statement but more a growth of buildings linking open spaces and courtyards to give a sense of surprise and delight as one wanders through the palace.

Built to accommodate the king and his extended family, there are many separate buildings spread out within the large compound wall. An independent dining hall near the entrance is meant for feeding a large number of Brahmins. The queen mother's house, situated just behind the king's living quarters, is said to be the oldest structure and has inside it famed carved pillars.

A large water tank at the rear is a delightful climax to the palace complex. It seems to give balance to the design. It is worth noting that the palace seems to gain a new enchantment on every visit especially

with its attention to detail and the use of simple materials. With
relatively simple forms the builders were able to achieve a blend of
grace and richness in its architecture.

At the rear of the complex, a comparatively new building has
been added. This was the guesthouse for European visitors. It can
be easily identified as it has high ceilings and is more colonial in style
and space. It, however, fits in well with the rest of the complex
without disturbing the design of the palace. The king had his chambers
in the middle of the complex and his bedroom in the tower that
can be seen from any part of the palace. The bedroom above his is
dedicated to Padmanabhaswami, the deity after whom the palace is
named. Although now empty, it has the most important paintings of
this era on its walls.

The Padmanabhapuram palace structures are an outstanding
example of the use of light and shade to achieve different moods
inside and outside. The council of chambers, for instance, is very dim
as one enters but as the eye adjusts, the space becomes well lit with
a subdued glow. An important feature in the chamber is a duct run-
ning under the seating area that allows air to circulate and cool the
room. Special herbs with gentle aromas were placed inside the duct.
These in turn enhanced the quality of air and even helped cure ail-
ments.

The craftsmanship of timber is creative throughout but it is in
the queen mother's palace that the intricacy is at its best. The vibrant
designs of the woodwork are in stark contrast to the austere
interiors that appear to be a feature of Kerala architecture.

The carpenters had to follow a strict code of rules and scale
when building and Padmanbhapuram is no exception. These rules,
obtained from the building shastras of Kerala, have kept the
continuity of design for more than a millennium. It is only in the
last century that buildings have gone out of proportion and seldom
please the eye.

The chamber for the
council of ministers is an
extraordinary room.

The entrance to the main
palace has an intricacy
which is seen in greater
detail inside.

196

Details of stained mica
windows in the chamber
for the council of
ministers.

The roofs of
Padmanabhapuram
palace. They appear
to be perfectly balanced
although the buildings
have been built at
different times.

The corridor surrounding the queen's palace is a good example of the way light is filtered into the rooms.

above Entrance to
the palace.

right The chamber of
council of ministers
seen from the outside.

left A view of the queen's palace seen from the main dining hall.

above Hanuman appears on one of the many gables.

above Main entrance court before entering the palace. The hills behind form a beautiful setting for this magnificent example of secular architecture.

right The king's room seen from the east. The room above his is the highest point in the palace and is reserved for Padmanabhaswami, the deity after whom the palace is named.

204

Detail of stone
on the tank wall.

The palace water supply is
from a large tank lined
with granite.

left An opening from a
small balcony-like room
overlooking the water
tank. Now closed, it is
perhaps one the finest
spaces in the palace.

Perumthrikkovil Sri Mahadeva Temple, Pazhoor

Devotees crossing the
river to go to the Pazhoor
temple.

SRI KRISHNA TEMPLE
Karatt

The Karatt temple in north Kerala is the simple version of a Kerala temple. Ronald Bernier in his book *Temple Arts of Kerala* feels this temple portrays a good example of the architecture created for this type of building. It is a small, well preserved shrine in the middle of the countryside. Almost lost in obscurity, it still has the srikovil adorned with murals. These are likely to disintegrate soon but still exemplify the art of painting in the temple tradition.

Built in laterite, the walls
are plastered and painted.
The mural shows Krishna
playing the flute.

Laterite stone has a warm texture and is relatively soft to work with. This image, taken with the evening light, gives some idea of the character of this material.

216 SRI KRISHNA TEMPLE
Tricchambaram

Trichambaram is a Krishna temple situated close to Taliparamba. It is very popular with the devotees of Krishna and normally has a festive air about it. Being an ancient temple it has some of the most interesting art depicting Krishna's exploits. Among the best known is his subjugation of Kaliya the serpent king, featured here.

A painted wooden bracket shows Krishna lifting the mountain at Govardhana when he saves the people from the flood brought on by the god Indra. The stucco work is crumbling but one can observe two pigeons peeping out close to the cows. The two bulls at his feet exhibit a sense of calm while the catastrophe is being averted.

Painted sculpture
depicting the destruction
of an Asura disguised as a
bird who tried to kill
Krishna.

Sri Vamanamoorthy Temple, Thrikkakara

Vamanamoorthy temple at
Thrikkakara is close to
Kochi and is dedicated
to the God Vamana (lord
of the south). It has little
decoration and the
simplicity of form makes
it different from the norm.
The clean lines bring a
freshness to the design.

222

'Whatever we cling to, even if it be hope or faith, can be a disease which carries us off. Surrender is absolute; if you cling to even the tiniest crumb you nourish the germ, which will devour you. As for clinging to God, God long ago abandoned us in order that we might realise the joy of attaining Godhood through our efforts.'

Henry Miller

Among the images that left a lasting impression was that of a pigeon taking shelter among the rafters. This is in contrast to the imperious eagle sitting on top of a stamba (brass pole) in front of the Rama temple. One is left with the question: Does one hide or fight as one goes through life's journey? It looks as if one is born to this indecision. Henry Miller (the American author) has clarified the question of faith which many of us face when visiting places of worship.

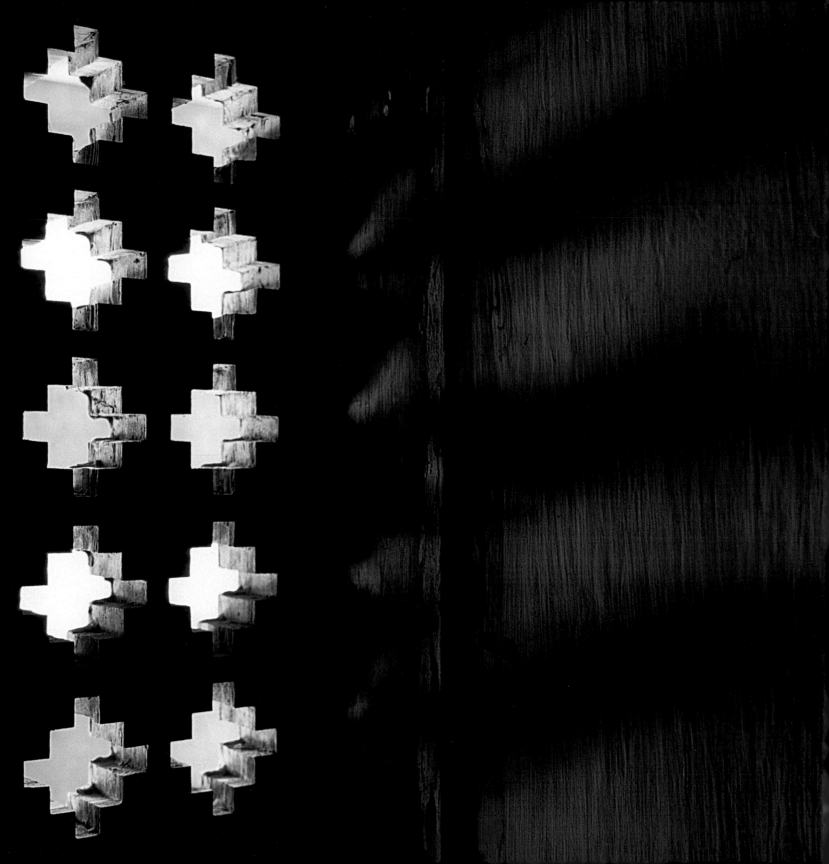

POSTSCRIPT

Although, outwardly, the temples are similar, each has its own identity. Some are on river banks while others in older settlements. The variation of the idols is also fascinating, especially in Siva temples where the image of Siva is usually in the abstract. The quality of the architecture in the temples of the Shankaracharaya period (8th century) is extraordinary while the majestic temples of the 17th century have developed a beautiful sense of space. The temples illustrated are the better known, but among the thousands to be seen, many will compare well with this selection. Just as one feels saturated with seeing temples, another gem will be spoken about and the visitor will be compelled to go there.

Restoration and preservation of the buildings are not taken as seriously as keeping the rituals of the temple intact. Sculpture of the highest order is allowed to decay and it is hoped this book is a start towards bringing awareness to the quality of artwork that is available. These illustrations are just the tip of the iceberg. It is hoped a future generation will recognize the value of this art and look after it.

Light filtering in through
a trellis into the
Koothambalam at
Vadakkunnatha temple.

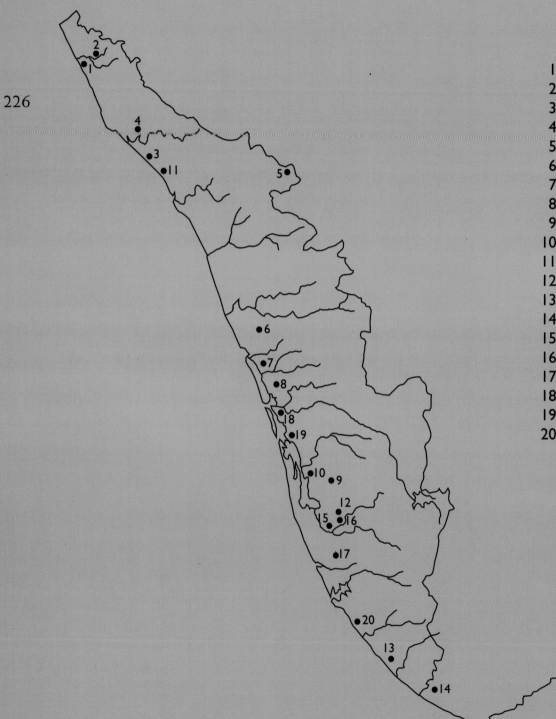

1. Kasargod
2. Anantha Padmanabhaswami
3. Kozhikode
4. Taliparamba
5. Thirunelli
6. Thrissur
7. Peruvanam
8. Irinjalakuda
9. Ettumanoor
10. Vaikom
11. Thiruvangad
12. Vazhapalli
13. Thiruvallam
14. Padmanabhapuram
15. Thiruvalla
16. Kaviyur
17. Krishnapuram
18. Thrikkakara
19. Thripoonithura
20. Varkala

Dashratha's soul being
carried on a heavenly
chariot. This panel
is just above the one that
depicts Rama's coronation
(page 146).

GLOSSARY

Bali-Peetha: Low stone pedestals sometimes covered with brass, positioned around the srikovil, representing various deities and used for oblation. These form a square around the srikovil and mark the cardinal directions.

Garbha-Griha: Sanctum sanctorum, the innermost chamber in the srikovil where the deity is installed.

Koothambalam: A rectangular hall of large size and exquisite proportions, capped by a pyramidal roof, located in the temple compound and used for sacred theatre. The columns, cornices and rafters made of wood are mostly carved with Vedic themes. It has a stage and greenrooms attached to the stage.

Namaskara Mandapa: A pillared pavilion sometimes positioned in the front of the srikovil where the priests pay their respects by prostration. The chanting of mantras and other temple rituals/prayers are also done from the Namaskara mandapa.

Srikovil: The main shrine in the inner court of a temple, the shape and size of which can vary from square, oblong, circular, elliptical to circular based on its geographical location in the state. The structure comprises of an innermost chamber (garbha-griha) in which the deity is installed. It may or may not have an ambulatory passage around the chamber. Also, depending upon its shape, the srikovil may have an ante-chamber or porch (mukha-mandapa) attached to it.

Sthambha/stamba: The flagstaff located mostly in front of the temple represents the vertebral column of the human body and is covered with metal sheeting. Covering materials may range from bell metal, brass and copper. The covering symbolizes the bones and the ribs around the spinal column. The stamba culminates with the deities' vaahana or transport, mostly an animal or bird. The deity is believed to be seated above the vaahana and therefore, the stamba is worshipped too.

SELECT BIBLIOGRAPHY

The Hindu Temple, Stella Kramrisch, University of Calcutta 1946
   re-published by Motilal Banarsidas, Delhi

The Arts and Crafts of Travancore, Stella Kramrisch, J H Cousins, R Vasudeva Poduval,
   Dept of Cultural Publications, Govt. of Kerala 1999, first published in 1948

An Architectural Survey of Temples of Kerala, H.Sarkar, Archaeological Survey
   of India 1978

Temple Architecture in Kerala, K.V.Soundarajan, Govt. of Kerala 1974

Temple Arts of Kerala, Ronald M. Bernier, S. Chand and Company 1982

Temples of Kerala, S. Jayashankar Census of India, Special Studies, Kerala 1997

Living Wood, Sculptural Traditions of Southern India, Edited by George Michell,
   Marg Publications 1992

The Blue Guide to Southern India, George Michell 1997

The Art of Indian Asia, Heinrich Zimmer Bollingen series, Princeton University 1955

232 ACKNOWLEDGEMENTS

I am grateful to the following people who have given their time and effort towards putting this book together:

Mammen and **Annamma Varghese** whose hospitality during the hot drives around Kottayam gave great comfort

Ranjit Kuruvilla our main contact in Thrissur

Wg.Cmd K. Parthasarthy (Partha) helped us getting many permissions in Malabar, north Kerala but more importantly was very enthusiastic about the book being completed.

Jacob Mathew(Chacko) unhesitatingly gave us accommodation when we needed it

Kaviyur Shivarama Aiyar a retired headmaster now in his eighties. His family bears the name Kaviyur and he belongs to the original Brahmins who settled here

Dr Sathi Nambiar organised our visit to the Rama temple in Thiruvangaad

P Ravindran helped us through the long sessions of photography at this temple

Joseph Pullikunnel owner of the wooden house featured

The Cochin Devaswom Board

Vinod Theancherry, architect, whose help was invaluable in Kannur

Suresh Babu for discovering the Pazhoor temple for us

A Pavanji for translating a Kannada booklet on Anantha Padmanabhaswami temple

Lakshmi Lal for useful suggestions and corrections

The Archaelogical Survey of India

The Travancore Devaswom Board without whose help most of the pictures would not have been possible

PHOTO CREDITS

NASA – Page 13

Ramu Katakam – Pages 2/3, 20/21, 23, 24/25, 34 (bottom right), 46, 58/59, 200/201, 202, 206/207